A Gift For:

Jan

From:

Phyl & Stan

For Better Days ♡

TRADE YOUR CARES FOR

Calm

BY MAX LUCADO

THOMAS NELSON
Since 1798

HarperCollins
PUBLISHERS
Since 1817

© 2017 Max Lucado

This edition published in 2018 by Hallmark Gift Books, a division of Hallmark Cards, Inc., Kansas City, MO 64141 under license from Thomas Nelson, a registered trademark of HarperCollins Christian Publishing, Inc.

Visit us on the Web at Hallmark.com.

Content is adapted from previously published material in *Anxious for Nothing*, *Before Amen*, *Come Thirsty*, *Facing Your Giants*, *Fearless*, *Glory Days*, *He Still Moves Stones*, *Max on Life*, *3:16: The Numbers of Hope*, *Traveling Light*, and *You'll Get Through This*.

Compiled by Allen Arnold

ISBN: 978-1-63059-737-5
1BOK1417

Made in China
0518

Denalyn and I happily dedicate this book to Tom and Silvia Cusick. Thank you for your friendship, generosity, and hospitality. Your mountain home provided the perfect setting to complete this book.

CONTENTS

INTRODUCTION

We aren't enjoying life as much as we used to. Concerns and worries rule our thoughts and actions. Potential for misfortune keeps us up at night. We worry about raising kids, mounting bills, the state of the country, and the state of our health. What-ifs and if-onlys collide to create a thunderstorm of fear. We feel like we are one crisis away from an emotional meltdown or panic attack.

Where can we turn? Or, better asked, to whom can we turn?

Henri Nouwen tells the story of a family of trapeze artists known as the Rodleighs. He traveled with the Rodleighs for a time, watching them fly through the air with elegant poise. When he asked one of the flyers the secret of successful acrobatic flight, the athlete gave this reply:

> The secret is that the flyer does nothing and the catcher does everything. When I fly . . . I have simply to stretch out my arms and hands and wait for Joe [my catcher] to catch me and pull me safely over the apron. . . . The worst thing the flyer can do is

to try to catch the catcher. I am not supposed to catch Joe. It's Joe's task to catch me. If I grabbed Joe's wrists, I might break them, or he might break mine, and that would be the end for both of us. A flyer must fly, and a catcher must catch, and the flyer must trust, with outstretched arms, that his catcher will be there for him.[1]

> IF YOU'VE BEEN TREMBLING ON A TIGHTROPE OF FEAR AND WORRY, MAY I SUGGEST THE BEST SOLUTION EVER? AN EXCHANGE: YOUR CARES FOR GOD'S CALM.

In the great trapeze act of salvation, God is the Catcher; we are the flyers. We trust. We rely solely upon God's ability to catch us. As we do, a wonderful thing happens: we find peace. We find joy. We find it is possible to be anxious for nothing.

If you've been trembling on a tightrope of fear and worry, may I suggest the best solution ever? A trade. An exchange: your cares for God's calm. You'll fly a lot freer without allowing worries to weigh you down. And in their place, you'll receive the Lord's mercy, goodness, and peace.

Are you ready to worry less and trust more? The path to peace is paved with prayer.

Rather than react to circumstances with clenched hands, reach out to the Father with outstretched arms. He's waiting to catch you, take hold of your anxieties, and in the process, trade your cares for his calm.

"Be anxious for nothing, but in everything by prayer and supplication, with thanksgiving, let your requests be made known to God; and the peace of God, which surpasses all understanding, will guard your hearts and minds through Christ Jesus" (Philippians 4:6–8).

Chapter 1

FACE FEAR AND ANXIETY

There's a stampede of fear out there. Let's not get caught in it. Let others breathe the polluted air of anxiety, not us. Let's be numbered among those who hear a different voice, God's. We will incline our ears upward. We will turn to our Maker, and because we do, we will fear less.

Fearless

FIGHT OR FLIGHT

It's a low-grade fear. An edginess, a dread. A cold wind that won't stop howling.

It's not so much a storm as it is the certainty that one is coming. Always . . . coming. Sunny days are just an interlude. You can't relax. Can't let your guard down. All peace is temporary, short-term.

So you don't sleep well.

You don't laugh often.

You don't enjoy the sun.

You don't whistle as you walk.

And when others do, you give them a look. *That* look. That "are you naive?" look. You may even give them a word. "Haven't you read the news and heard the reports and seen the studies?"

Airplanes fall out of the sky. Bull markets go bear. Terrorists terrorize. Good people turn bad. The other shoe will drop. Fine print will be found. Misfortune lurks out there; it's just a matter of time.

Anxiety and fear are cousins but not twins. Fear sees a threat. Anxiety imagines one.

Fear screams, *Get out!*

Anxiety ponders, *What if?*

Could you use some calm? God is ready to give it.

With God as your helper, you will sleep better tonight and smile more tomorrow. You'll reframe the way you face your fears. You'll learn how to talk yourself off the ledge, view bad news through the lens of sovereignty, discern the lies of Satan, and tell yourself the truth.

Anxiety comes with life. But it doesn't have to dominate your life.

> ANXIETY COMES WITH LIFE.
> BUT IT DOESN'T HAVE TO
> DOMINATE YOUR LIFE.

GOD'S WORDS OF PEACE

*C*ould you use some calm? If so, you aren't alone. The Bible is Kindle's most highlighted book. And Philippians 4:6–7 is the most highlighted passage.[2] Apparently we could all use these words of peace, so let's go through these words slowly, letting each find its way to our hearts.

> Rejoice in the Lord always. Again I will say, rejoice! Let your gentleness be known to all men. The Lord is at hand. Be anxious for nothing, but in everything by prayer and supplication, with thanksgiving, let your requests be made known to God; and the peace of God, which surpasses all understanding, will guard your hearts and minds through Christ Jesus.
>
> Finally, brethren, whatever things are true, whatever things are noble, whatever things are just, whatever things are pure, whatever things are lovely, whatever things are

of good report, if there is any virtue and if there is anything praiseworthy—meditate on these things.

—*Philippians 4:4–8*

Five verses with four admonitions that lead to one wonderful
promise: "the peace of God, which surpasses all understanding,
will guard your hearts and minds" (v. 7).

Celebrate God's goodness. "Rejoice in the Lord always" (v. 4).
Ask God for help. "Let your requests be made known to
    God" (v. 6).
Leave your concerns with him. "With thanksgiving . . ."
    (v. 6).
Meditate on good things. "Think about the things that are
    good and worthy of praise" (v. 8 NCV).

Celebrate. Ask. Leave. Meditate. C.A.L.M.

BE ANXIOUS FOR NOTHING

*C*hances are that you or someone you know seriously struggles with anxiety. According to the National Institute of Mental Health, anxiety disorders are reaching epidemic proportions. "The United States is now the most anxious nation in the world."[3] (Congratulations to us!) The land of the Stars and Stripes has become the country of stress and strife.

It's enough to make us wonder if the apostle Paul was out of touch with reality when he wrote, "Be anxious for nothing" (Philippians 4:6).

"Be anxious for less" would have been a sufficient challenge. Or "Be anxious only on Thursdays." Or "Be anxious only in seasons of severe affliction."

THE PRESENCE OF ANXIETY IS UNAVOIDABLE, BUT THE PRISON OF ANXIETY IS OPTIONAL.

But Paul doesn't seem to offer any leeway here. Be anxious for nothing. Nada. Zilch. Zero. Is this what he meant? Not exactly. He wrote the phrase in the present active tense, which implies an ongoing state. It's the life of *perpetual anxiety* that Paul wanted to address. The *Lucado Revised Translation* reads, "Don't let anything in life leave you perpetually breathless and in angst." The presence of anxiety is unavoidable, but the prison of anxiety is optional.

Anxiety is not a sin; it is an emotion. (So, don't be anxious about feeling anxious.) Anxiety can, however, lead to sinful behavior. When we treat our worries with inebriation or angry outbursts, we are sinning. For that reason, Jesus gave this word: "Be careful, or your hearts will be weighed down with . . . the anxieties of life" (Luke 21:34 NIV).

COPING STRATEGIES

Some coping strategies are healthy; others are counter-productive. An important step for assembling good tools is identifying the bad ones. Which coping strategies do you use?

When I am anxious, I:

___ try to relax

___ seek advice and assurance from a trusted friend

___ take prescription medication

___ suppress my feelings

___ busy myself with activities unrelated to my problem (e.g. working in the garden)

___ get angry

___ have a smoke

___ pray, meditate, read Scripture

___ try to understand the source of my worry

___ other _____

Evaluate your list. Are your coping methods, by and large, good ones? Or does your response to anxiety create even more problems?

GOD IS IN ALL DAYS

Suppose the wife of George Frideric Handel came upon a page of her husband's famous oratorio *Messiah*. The entire work was more than two hundred pages long. Imagine that she discovered one page on the kitchen table. On it her husband had written only one measure in a minor key, one that didn't work on its own. Suppose she, armed with this fragment of dissonance, marched into his studio and said, "This music makes no sense. You are a lousy composer." What would he think?

Perhaps something similar to what God thinks when we do the same. We point to our minor key—our sick child, crutches, or famine—and say, "This makes no sense!" Yet out of all God's creations, how much have we seen? And of all his work, how much do we understand? Only a sliver. A doorway peephole. Is it possible that some explanation for suffering exists of which we know nothing at all? What if God's answer to the question of suffering requires more megabytes than our puny minds have been given?

And is it possible that the wonder of heaven will make the most difficult life a good bargain? This was Paul's opinion. "Our light and momentary troubles are achieving for us an eternal glory that far outweighs them all" (2 Corinthians 4:17 NIV).

What is coming will make sense of what is happening now. Let God finish his work. Let the composer complete his symphony. The forecast is simple.

IS IT POSSIBLE THAT THE WONDER OF HEAVEN WILL MAKE THE MOST DIFFICULT LIFE A GOOD BARGAIN?

Good days. Bad days. But God is in all days. He is the Lord of the famine and the feast, and he uses both to accomplish his will.

LEARN THE MESSAGE

OF THE MANNA

God promised to supply Moses and the Hebrews with manna each day. But he told them to collect only one day's supply at a time. Those who disobeyed and collected enough for two days found themselves with rotten manna. The only exception to the rule was the day prior to the Sabbath. On Friday, they could gather twice as much. In other words, God gave them what they needed in their time of need. "Give your entire attention to what God is doing right now, and don't get worked up about what may or may not happen tomorrow. God will help you deal with whatever hard things come up when the time comes" (Matthew 6:34 MSG).

Doesn't each day have its share of challenges? Some of them repeat themselves over time; others are one-day specials. The key to tranquility is to face today's problems and no more, to treat each day like a self-contained unit. Here are today's problems. Meet them with God's strength. But don't start tackling tomorrow's problems until tomorrow. You do not have tomorrow's strength yet. You simply have enough for today. You can't cross a bridge until you reach it.

- **Find a parking place for tomorrow's problems.** When they surface, write them down and mentally drive them into a parking garage and leave them there.
- **Don't overstress your coping skills.** Emotional energy is finite. Give yourself permission to say, "I will solve this tomorrow. By sunrise I will be replenished physically and mentally. Every day is a fresh start so I will start fresh in the morning."
- **Shut the gate on yesterday, and don't touch the gate on tomorrow.** "This is the day the LORD has made; we will rejoice and be glad in it" (Psalm 118:24). You no longer have yesterday. You do not yet have tomorrow. You only have today. Live in it!

EVERYTHING IS SECURE

My father had a bedtime routine that makes me smile to think about. He loved corn bread and buttermilk. (Can you guess that I was raised in a small West Texas town?) About ten o'clock each night, he would meander into the kitchen, crumble a piece of corn bread into a glass of buttermilk, and drink it.

He then made the rounds to the front and back doors, checking the locks. Once everything was secure, he would step into the bedroom I shared with my brother and say something like, "Everything is secure, boys. You can go to sleep now."

I have no inclination to believe that God loves corn bread and buttermilk, but I do believe he loves his children. He oversees your world. He monitors your life. He doesn't need to check the doors; indeed, he is the door. Nothing will come your way apart from his permission.

Listen carefully and you will hear him say, "Everything is secure. You can rest now." By his power you will "be anxious for nothing . . ." and discover the "peace . . . which passes all understanding" (Philippians 4:6–7 RSV).

MEDITATE ON THESE THINGS

*I*t helps when we take our eyes off the problems and fix them on God. That's why Paul told us in Philippians 4 to meditate on godly things. Take a moment and list the things in the world—and your life—that are:

Noble: _____

Just: _____

Pure: _____

Lovely: _____

Of good report: _____

Virtuous: _____

Praiseworthy: _____

Chapter 2

WALK AWAY FROM WORRY

Imagine your whole life untouched by worry. What if faith, not fear, were your default reactions to threats? Envision a day, just one, absent the dread of failure, rejection, and calamity. This is the possibility behind Jesus' question, "Why are you afraid?" (Matthew 8:26 NCV).

Fearless

FEAR LESS TOMORROW

Fear may fill our world, but it doesn't have to fill our hearts. It will always knock on the door. Just don't invite it in for dinner, and for heaven's sake, don't offer it a bed for the night. The promise of Christ is simple: we can fear less tomorrow than we do today.

When I was six years old, my dad let me stay up late with the rest of the family and watch the movie *The Wolf Man*. Boy, did he regret that decision. The film left me convinced that the Wolf Man spent each night prowling our den, awaiting his preferred meal of first-grade, red-headed, freckle-salted boy. My fear proved problematic.

WE CAN FEAR LESS TOMORROW THAN WE DO TODAY.

To reach the kitchen from my bedroom, I had to pass perilously close to his claws and fangs, something I was loath to do. More than once I retreated to my father's bedroom and awoke him. Like Jesus on the boat, Dad was sound asleep in the storm. *How can a person sleep at a time like this?*

Opening a sleepy eye, he would ask, "Now, why are you

afraid?" And I would remind him of the monster. "Oh yes, the Wolf Man," he'd grumble. He would then climb out of bed, arm himself with super-human courage, escort me through the valley of the shadow of death, and pour me a glass of milk. I would look at him with awe and wonder, *What kind of man is this?*

Might it be that God views our storms the way my father viewed my Wolf Man angst? "Jesus got up and gave a command to the wind and the waves, and it became completely calm" (Matthew 8:26 NCV).

He handles the great quaking with great calm. The sea becomes as still as a frozen lake, and the disciples are left wondering, "What kind of man is this? Even the wind and the waves obey him!" (Matthew 8:27 NCV).

What kind of man indeed.

The LORD

is my

light and

my *salvation*;

whom shall

I fear?

PSALM 27:1

GOD'S WORD FOR YOUR WORRIES

"So don't be afraid. You are worth much more than many sparrows."

—*Matthew* 10:31 NCV

"I tell you not to worry about everyday life."

—*Matthew* 6:25 NLT

"Take courage. I am here!"

—*Matthew* 14:27 NLT

"Do not fear those who kill the body but are unable to kill the soul."

—*Matthew* 10:28 NASB

"Do not be afraid, little flock, for your Father has chosen gladly to give you the kingdom."

—*Luke 12:32 NASB*

"Don't let your hearts be troubled. Trust in God, and trust also in me . . . I will come and get you, so that you will always be with me where I am."

—*John 14:1, 3 NLT*

EVALUATE YOUR WORRY PATTERNS

This week make a note every time you feel anxious. Observe some details about your troubling thoughts.

- What were you worried about?
- What situation or event triggered the anxiety?
- How did this anxiety make you feel?
- How did you react?

Take a few minutes to review what you have observed about your worries.

- Try to identify the core fear or insecurity behind the anxiety. Do you see a common theme? Is there some catastrophic event you fear?
- How many of your worries materialized? Highlight the number of times you were worried about something that never actually happened.

- Was the gain worth the pain? As you look at the emotional toll the anxiety took, was it worth it?
- How did your anxiety affect others in your life?
- Is there anything you can do to address the source of anxiety? What is a practical step you can take? Make an intentional choice to act so that the next time this anxiety surfaces, you can tell yourself what you are doing to alleviate the potential problem.
- Each morning add your concern to your prayer time. Ask God to go ahead of you.

TEMPORARY LIMPS

Want to win the war on worry? Begin with the admiration of God. Rejoice in the Lord's strength, faithfulness, and accomplishments. Rejoice in his creation, his incarnation, and his act of redemption. As you do, you reinforce your faith. Anxiety decreases as our understanding of the Lord increases.

Think of it this way. Suppose your dad is the world's foremost orthopedic surgeon. People travel from distant countries for him to treat them. With the same confidence that a mechanic changes spark plugs, your dad removes and replaces hips, knees, and shoulders.

ANXIETY DECREASES AS OUR UNDERSTANDING OF THE LORD INCREASES.

At ten years of age, you are a bit young to comprehend the accomplishments of a renowned surgeon. But you're not too young to stumble down the stairs and twist your ankle. You are weeks away from your first school dance. This is no time for crutches. No time for limping.

Into the room walks your dad, still wearing his surgical scrubs.

"Dad, I'll never walk again!"

"Yes, you will."

"No one can help me!"

"I can."

"No one knows what to do!"

"I do."

"No, you don't!"

Your dad lifts his head and asks you a question. "Do you know what I do for a living?"

Actually, you don't. You know he goes to the hospital every day. But you don't really know what your father does.

"So," he says as he places a bag of ice on your ankle, "it's time for you to learn." The next day you have a ringside seat for a procedure in which he reconstructs a patient's ankle. He is the commandant of the operating room. He never hesitates or seeks advice. He just does it.

As the two of you ride home that evening, you look at your father. You see him in a different light. If he can conduct orthopedic surgery, he can likely treat a swollen ankle. So you ask, "You think I'll be okay for the dance?"

"Yes, you'll be fine."

This time you believe him. Your anxiety decreases as your understanding of your father increases.

Here is what I think: our biggest fears are sprained ankles to God.

Here is what else I think: a lot of people live with unnecessary anxiety over temporary limps.

WEIGH YOUR WORRIES

Want to see if your heart is weighed down with worry? Look for these clues:

_____ Are you laughing less than you once did?
_____ Do you see problems in every promise?
_____ Would those who know you best describe you as increasingly negative and critical?
_____ Do you assume that something bad is going to happen?
_____ Many days would you rather stay in bed than get up?
_____ Do you magnify the negative and dismiss the positive?
_____ If given the chance, would you avoid any interaction with humanity for the rest of your life?

If you answered yes to more than a few of these questions, the Prince of Peace stands ready to help trade your cares for calm.

WORRY BUSTERS

Try these eight powerful worry-stoppers.

1. Pray first. Don't pace up and down the floors of the waiting room; pray for successful surgery. Don't bemoan the collapse of an investment; ask God to help you. "Let him have all your worries and cares" (1 Peter 5:7 TLB).

2. Easy, now. Slow down. "Rest in the LORD and wait patiently for Him" (Psalm 37:7 NASB).

3. Act on it. Become a worry-slapper. Treat frets like mosquitoes. Give them the slap they deserve. Be equally decisive with anxiety. The moment a concern surfaces, deal with it rather than dwell on it.

4. Compile a worry list. Over a period of days, record your anxious thoughts. Then review them later. How many of them turned into a reality? Likely few, if any.

5. Evaluate your worry categories. Your list will highlight themes of worry. Detect recurring areas of preoccupation that may become obsessions—and pray specifically about them.

6. Focus on today. God meets needs daily. Not weekly or annually. He will give you what you need when you need it. "Let us come boldly to the throne of our gracious God. There we will receive his mercy, and we will find grace to help us when we need it most" (Hebrews 4:16 NLT).

7. Unleash a worry army. Share your feelings with a few loved ones. Ask them to pray with and for you. They're more willing to help than you might imagine. Less worry on your part means more happiness on theirs.

8. Let God be enough. Jesus concludes his call to calmness with this challenge: "Your heavenly Father already knows all your needs. Seek the Kingdom of God above all else, and live righteously, and he will give you everything you need" (Matthew 6:32–33 NLT).

Eight steps. Pray first. Easy, now. Act on it. Compile a worry list. Evaluate your worry categories. Focus on today. Unleash a worry army. Let God be enough.

Put them together and you get P-E-A-C-E-F-U-L.

GOD IS BIGGER

*I*n the book *Prince Caspian*, Lucy sees Aslan, the lion, for the first time in many years. He has changed since their last encounter. His size surprises her, and she tells him as much.

> "Aslan," said Lucy, "you're bigger."
> "That is because you are older, little one," he answered.
> "Not because you are?"
> "I am not. But every year you grow, you will find me bigger."[4]

And so it is with Christ. The longer we live in him, the greater he becomes in us. It's not that he changes but that we do; we see more of him. We see dimensions, aspects, and characteristics we never saw before, increasing and astonishing increments of his purity, power, and uniqueness.

JOURNALING YOUR WORRIES

1. What are you most afraid of, and why?

2. Can you imagine going through an entire day without any worries? Why does it seem so hard to walk away from what worries you most?

3. "Anxiety decreases as our understanding of the Lord increases." What are ways your understanding of Jesus might increase even more?

4. List three worries that you are giving to Jesus right now. Do you believe he can free you from their power?

Chapter 3

CONQUER CONTROL

God's answer for troubled times has always been the same: heaven has an occupied throne.

Anxious for Nothing

FUEL-FILLED FAITH

Trying to control all the details of your world is exhausting. And for good reason. Only God has the power to see and know everything. But we forget. And before long, we're back at it—running too fast, working too many hours, and trying to control everyone and everything around us.

The question isn't if this approach will wear you out. It's what do you do when you run out of gas?

Stare at the gauge? Blame your upbringing? Deny the problem? Never works.

In the case of an empty tank, we've learned: get the car to a gas pump ASAP. In life, we try to push the car ourselves. We are in such a hurry to get where we want to go that we scoff at the service station, get out of the driver's seat, and try to do things with our own effort. Push, push, push. Stopping for gas is for wimps.

If you are putting in sixty hours a week to build up your "own" business, that may signal you are pushing the car yourself. And you're likely getting tired.

To avoid suffering from a fuel-less faith, you need to fill

yourself with some high-test fuel. Try some Philippians—six promises from a premium-grade book.

- Being confident of this, that he who began a good work in you will carry it on to completion until the day of Christ Jesus. (1:6 NIV)
- For to me, to live is Christ and to die is gain. (1:21 NIV)
- Do nothing out of selfish ambition or vain conceit. Rather, in humility value others above yourselves. (2:3 NIV)
- I want to know Christ—yes, to know the power of his resurrection and participation in his sufferings, becoming like him in his death. (3:10 NIV)
- I press on toward the goal to win the prize for which God has called me heavenward in Christ Jesus. (3:14 NIV)
- I can do all this through him who gives me strength. (4:13 NIV)

Fill your tank with verses like these, and stop trying to push yourself around. And remember: God is able to do what you can't.

Being *confident* of this,

that he who began

a good work in you

will carry it on to

completion until the

day of Christ Jesus.

TELL YOURSELF THE TRUTH

The first word on Paul's meditation list in Philippians 4:8 is *true*. We waste so much nervous energy trying to make decisions. Rather than becoming overwhelmed and immobilized or hypervigilant and controlling, we can stress less when we remember three things.

Gather the facts. How many planes actually fall out of the sky? How many bridges actually collapse? How many people die from the disease you dread? Examine the record. What are the odds that the thing you are worrying about will ever occur?

Control what you can control. Once you know precisely the challenge that faces you, make a list of what you can do about it. Weather? You can't control it. (But you can watch the forecast.) The economy? You can't control it. (But you can keep a budget and live within your means.) Your boss's opinion of you? You can't control it. (But you can influence it by doing your work and not worrying about everyone else's.)

Don't second-guess yourself. It does no good to do so. Make the best decision you can with the facts at hand, and live with it. Pray and take the next step.

RELINQUISHING CONTROL

When you can't sleep, don't count sheep—read Scripture. Distinguish between God's voice and the voice of fear.

Worry takes a look at catastrophes and groans, "It's all coming unraveled."

God says, "Every detail in our lives of love for God is worked into something good" (Romans 8:28 MSG).

Worry claims, "The world has gone crazy."

God's Word disagrees: "[Jesus has] done it all and done it well" (Mark 7:37 MSG).

Worry wonders if anyone is in control.

God's Word calls God "the blessed controller of all things" (1 Timothy 6:15 PHILLIPS).

Worry whispers this lie: "God doesn't know what I need."

God's Word declares, "God will take care of everything you need" (Philippians 4:19 MSG).

Worry never sleeps.

WE CAN'T TAKE CONTROL BECAUSE CONTROL IS NOT OURS TO TAKE.

God's children do.

The formula is simple: perceived control creates calm. Lack of control gives birth to fear. Anxiety increases as perceived control diminishes.

So what do we do?

Control everything? Never board a plane without a parachute. Never enter a restaurant without bringing your own clean silverware. Never leave the house without a gas mask. Never give away your heart for fear of a broken one. Some people face anxiety by taking control.

If only we could.

Yet, certainty is a cruel imposter. A person can accumulate millions of dollars and still lose it in a recession. A health fanatic can eat only nuts and veggies and still battle cancer. A hermit can avoid all human contact and still struggle with insomnia. We want certainty, but the only certainty is the lack thereof.

That's why the most stressed-out people are control freaks. They fail at the quest they most pursue. We can't take control because control is not ours to take.

The Bible has a better idea. Rather than seeking total control, relinquish it. You can't run the world, but you can entrust it to God.

GOD'S WORDS ON CONQUERING CONTROL

Do nothing out of selfish ambition or vain conceit. Rather, in humility value others above yourselves.

—Philippians 2:3 NIV

I want to know Christ—yes, to know the power of his resurrection and participation in his sufferings, becoming like him in his death.

—Philippians 3:10 NIV

I press on toward the goal to win the prize for which God has called me heavenward in Christ Jesus.

—Philippians 3:14 NIV

I can do all this through him who gives me strength.

—Philippians 4:13 NIV

CONTROLLING THE FUTURE

You might think that even the most controlling among us would realize the one thing absolutely out of their control would be the end of the world. But even that doesn't stop some folks from trying.

A recent article by the *Associated Press* reveals that Texas investors are building a $300 million luxury bunker community for just such a doomsday scenario.[5] It's the perfect place for those worried about a dirty bomb or other catastrophic event.

Overlooking the new development will stand a fifty-foot statue of Poseidon, the Greek god of the sea, gripping his trident some fifty feet atop one of the largest fountains in the world.

To keep residents immune from any unpleasant ramifications from our world imploding, the community plans an eighteen-hole golf course, luxury shops, an equestrian center, polo fields, a twenty-acre lake with man-made white sand beaches, a high-end spa, and zip lines. But that's only for the high-paying residents. The rest of us will find ourselves on the outside of the twelve-foot walls and security watchtowers surrounding the community.

The one thing residents might miss is the morning sunrise, since ninety percent of their living space will be underground behind secure air-lock blast doors.

The high-end, end-times community may be to die for . . . but the goal is that you never will die in it. Should someone "expire" while there, the community is creating DNA vaults for "family sustainability." Which means should Uncle Gus not wake up one day, he can simply be "replicated"—hopefully before morning tee time.

Humans will go to any extreme to control their destiny. And yet God makes clear that only he controls the future. "We plan the way we want to live, but only God makes us able to live it" (Proverbs 16:9 MSG).

If we can trust God with the next twenty-four hours, we'll tend to worry less about our final twenty-four hours. God offers us something far better than an escape from the future. He offers himself.

"WE PLAN THE WAY WE WANT TO LIVE, BUT ONLY GOD MAKES US ABLE TO LIVE IT" (PROVERBS 16:9 MSG).

A LINE IN THE SAND

Are we in control, or is God? For my friends Brian and Christyn Taylor, the question is more than academic. During the course of one year, their seven-year-old daughter was hospitalized for more than six months with six surgeries. Brian's job was discontinued, several family members died and another was diagnosed with brain cancer, and Christyn was pregnant with their fourth child. Life was tough. She blogged:

> God and I had a deal—I would endure the trials that came my way as long as he acknowledged my stopping point. He knew where my line had been drawn, and I knew in my heart that he would never cross it.
>
> He did. I delivered a stillborn baby girl. With my daughter Rebecca still at home on a feeding tube and her future health completely unknown, it was a foregone conclusion that this baby we so wanted and loved would be saved. She wasn't. My line in the sand was crossed. My one-way deal with God was shattered.
>
> Everything changed in that moment. Fear set in, and my

faith began to crumble. My "safety zone" with God was no longer safe. If this could happen in the midst of our greatest struggles, then anything was fair game. For the first time in my life, anxiety began to overwhelm me.[6]

Ultimately, our choice comes down to this: trust God or turn away. He will cross the line. He will shatter our expectations. And we will be left to make a decision.

Christyn Taylor made hers. She concluded her blog with these words:

I have spent weeks trying to figure out why a God I so love could let this happen to my family at such a time. The only conclusion I came to was this: I have to give up my line in the sand. I have to offer my entire life, every minute portion of it, to God's control regardless of the outcome.

My family is in God's hands. No lines have been drawn, no deals made. I have given our lives to the Lord. Peace has entered where panic once resided, and calmness settled where anxiety once ruled.

TRUST HIM

Many years ago I spent a week visiting the interior of Brazil with an experienced missionary pilot. He flew a circuit of remote towns in a four-seat plane that threatened to come undone at the slightest gust of wind. Wilbur and Orville had a sturdier aircraft.

I could not get comfortable. I kept thinking that the plane was going to crash in some Brazilian jungle and I'd be gobbled up by piranhas or swallowed by an anaconda. I kept shifting around, looking down, and gripping my seat. (As if that would help.)

Finally, the pilot had enough of my squirming. He looked over at me and shouted over the airplane noise, "We won't face anything that I can't handle. You might as well trust me to fly the plane."

Is God saying the same to you?

JOURNALING AWAY CONTROL

1. In what area of life do you feel the need to control?

2. Review the list. How many of those outcomes do you truly control—meaning it is absolutely and totally within your power to make them happen?

3. Which of the things you have worried about have come to fruition?

Try this prayer to help you relinquish the illusion of control.

Dear Lord,

You are perfect. You could not be better than you are.

You are self-created. You exist because you choose to exist.

You are self-sustaining. No one helps you. No one gives you strength.

You are self-governing. Who can question your deeds? Who dares advise you?

You are correct. In every way. In every choice. You regret no decision.

You have never failed. Never! You cannot fail! You are God! You will accomplish your plan.

You are happy. Eternally joyful. Endlessly content.

You are the king, supreme ruler, absolute monarch, and overlord of all history.

An arch of your eyebrow and a million angels will pivot and salute. Every throne is a footstool to yours. Every crown is papier-mâché next to yours. No limitations, hesitations, questions, second thoughts, or backward glances. You consult no clock. You keep no calendar. You report to no one. You are in charge.

And I trust you.

Chapter 4

SEE GOD'S GOODNESS

Don't get lost in your troubles. Dare to believe good things will happen. Dare to believe that God was speaking to you when he said, "In everything God works for the good of those who love him" (Romans 8:28 NCV). God is working for your good. And you are in his strong and mighty hands.

Anxious for Nothing

FILLED WITH GOD'S GOODNESS

Kent Brantly was a medical missionary in Liberia, waging a war on the cruelest of viruses, Ebola. The epidemic was killing people by the thousands. He had treated dozens of cases. He knew the symptoms—soaring fever, severe diarrhea, and nausea. He had seen the results of the virus, and for the first time he was feeling the symptoms himself.

His colleagues had drawn blood and begun the tests. But it would be at least three days before they knew the results. Dr. Brantly quarantined himself in his house and waited. His wife and family were across the ocean. His coworkers could not enter his residence. He was, quite literally, alone with his thoughts.

He opened his Bible and meditated on a passage from the book of Hebrews. Then he wrote in his journal, "Let us, therefore, approach the throne of grace with confidence, so that we may receive mercy and find grace to help us in our time of need" (Hebrews 4:16 NIV, 1984 edition).

The next three days brought unspeakable discomfort. The test results confirmed what they feared: he had contracted Ebola.

Kent called his wife, Amber, with the diagnosis. "The test results came back. It's positive."

Now it was Amber's turn to process the news. She found it difficult to find words to formulate her prayers, so she used the lyrics of hymns she had learned as a young girl.

She later wrote, "I thought my husband was going to die. I was in pain. I was afraid. Through those hymns, though, I was able to connect with God in a meaningful way when I couldn't find my own words to pray."[7]

Kent was transported from Africa to Atlanta. His caregivers chose to risk an untested treatment. Within a few days his strength began to return. The entire world, it seemed, rejoiced when he was able to exit the hospital, cured of Ebola.

We can applaud Kent and Amber's victory over another disease, a virus that is every bit as deadly and contagious: the unseen contagion of anxiety. They were prime candidates for panic, yet they reacted with the same resolve that enabled them to battle Ebola. Kent opened his Bible. Amber meditated on hymns. They filled their minds with the goodness of God.

May we do the same.

GOD IS FOR YOU

God is good. But it gets even better. He is for you.

And "If God is for us, who can be against us?" (Romans 8:31). From his perspective, you are worth the death of his Son. You are valuable, purposeful, and important. "Fear not, for I have redeemed you; I have called you by name, you are mine" (Isaiah 43:1 RSV).

If God is for you, shouldn't you be for you? Does it make sense for you to be against you? You are against you when you call yourself dumb, ugly, or poor. You are against you when you tell yourself that there is no solution, hope, or promise in life. You are against you when you decide that you have no talents or friends or future.

So how do you begin to see yourself as God does?

Remember that your words matter. You are either your worst critic or greatest cheerleader. The words you tell yourself will either usher in fear or faith. "The soothing tongue is a tree of life, but a perverse tongue crushes the spirit" (Proverbs 15:4 NIV).

Hold fast to the promises of scripture. Tell yourself the truth about yourself. The apostle Paul modeled this for us. "No, in all these things we are more than conquerors through him who loved us. For I am convinced that neither death nor life, neither angels nor demons, neither the present nor the future, nor any powers, neither height nor depth, nor anything else in all creation, will be able to separate us from the love of God that is in Christ Jesus our Lord" (Romans 8:37–39 NIV).

Personalize that passage. Insert the sources of anxiety that come your way. "No, in all these things we are more than conquerors through him who loved us. For I am convinced that neither *poor health,* neither *college debt* nor *pink slips,* neither today's *deadline* nor *tomorrow's diagnosis,* nor any *job transfers,* neither *addictions* nor *moral failures,* nor anything else in all creation, will be able to separate me from the love of God that is in Christ Jesus our Lord."

Be for you! God is.

REMEMBER GOD'S BLESSINGS

*J*esus performed two bread-multiplying miracles: in one he fed 5,000 people, in the other 4,000. Still his disciples, who witnessed both feasts, worried about empty pantries. A frustrated Jesus rebuked them: "Are your hearts too hard to take it in? . . . Don't you remember anything at all?" (Mark 8:17–18 NLT).

Short memories harden the heart. Make careful note of God's blessings. Declare with David: "[I will] daily add praise to praise. I'll write the book on your righteousness, talk up your salvation the livelong day, never run out of good things to write or say" (Psalm 71:14–15 MSG).

Catalog God's goodness. Meditate on his work. He has fed you, led you, and earned your trust. Remember what God has done for you.

IS GOD ALWAYS GOOD?

Is God only good when the outcome is?

When the illness is in remission, we say "God is good." When the pay raise comes, we announce "God is good." When the university admits us or the final score favors our team, "God is good." Would we—and do we—say the same under different circumstances? In the cemetery as well as the nursery? In the unemployment line as well as the grocery line? In days of recession as much as in days of provision? Is God always good?

Most of us have a contractual agreement with God. The fact that he hasn't signed it doesn't keep us from believing it.

I pledge to be a good, decent person, and in return, God will . . .

save my child.
heal my wife.
protect my job.
(fill in the blank) _____

Only fair, right? Yet when God fails to meet our bottom-line expectations, we are left spinning in a tornado of questions. Is he good at all? Is God angry at me? Stumped? Overworked? Is his power limited? His authority restricted? Did the devil outwit him?

When life isn't good, what are we to think about God? Where is he in all this?

At some point, we all stand at this intersection. Is God good when the outcome is not? During the famine as well as the feast? The definitive answer comes in the person of Jesus Christ. He is the only picture of God ever taken. Do you want to know heaven's clearest answer to the question of suffering? Look at Jesus.

He pressed fingers into the sore of the leper. He wept at the death of a friend. He stopped his work to tend to the needs of a grieving mother. He doesn't recoil, run, or retreat at the sight of pain. Just the opposite. He didn't walk the earth in an insulated bubble or preach from an isolated, germfree, pain-free island. Trivial irritations of family life? Jesus felt them. Cruel accusations of jealous men? Jesus knew their sting. A seemingly senseless death? Just look at the cross. He exacts nothing from us that he did not experience himself.

Why? Because he is good.

> DO YOU WANT TO KNOW HEAVEN'S CLEAREST ANSWER TO THE QUESTION OF SUFFERING? LOOK AT JESUS.

Your goal is not to

know every detail

of the future.

Your goal is to

hold the hand of

the One who does

and never, ever let go.

ANXIOUS FOR NOTHING

WHILE YOU WAIT

Are you in God's waiting room? Perhaps you are between jobs or in search of health, help, a house, or a spouse. If so, here is what you need to know: *while you wait, God works.*

"My Father is always at his work," Jesus said (John 5:17 NIV). God never twiddles his thumbs. He never stops. He takes no vacations. He rested on the seventh day of creation but got back to work on the eighth and hasn't stopped since. Just because you are idle, don't assume God is.

"Be still and know that I am God" reads the sign on God's waiting room wall. You can be glad because God is good. You can be still because he is active. You can rest because he is busy.

Remember God's word through Moses to the Israelites? "Do not be afraid. Stand still, and see the salvation of the LORD . . . The LORD will fight for you, and you shall hold your peace" (Exodus 14:13–14). The Israelites saw the

> GOD NEVER TWIDDLES HIS THUMBS. HE NEVER STOPS. HE TAKES NO VACATIONS.

Red Sea ahead of them and heard the Egyptian soldiers thundering after them.

Death on both sides. *Stand still? Are you kidding?* But what the former slaves couldn't see was the hand of God at the bottom of the water, creating a path, and his breath from heaven, separating the waters. God was working for them.

God worked for Mary, the mother of Jesus. The angel told her that she would become pregnant. The announcement stirred a torrent of questions in her heart. How would she become pregnant? What would people think? What would Joseph say? Yet God was working for her. He sent a message to Joseph, her fiancé. God prompted Caesar to declare a census. God led the family to Bethlehem. "God is always at work for the good of everyone who loves him" (Romans 8:28 CEV).

To wait, biblically speaking, is not to assume the worst, worry, fret, make demands, or take control. Nor is waiting inactivity. Waiting is a sustained effort to stay focused on God through prayer and belief. To wait is to "rest in the LORD, and wait patiently for Him" (Psalm 37:7).

ABIDING IN HIM

How do we disarm anxiety? Stockpile our minds with God thoughts. Saturate your heart with the goodness of God. "Set your mind on things above, not on things on the earth" (Colossians 3:2). How might you do this?

A friend recently described to me her daily ninety-minute commute.

"Ninety minutes!" I commiserated.

"Don't feel sorry for me." She smiled. "I use the trip to think about God." She went on to describe how she fills the hour and a half with worship and sermons. She listens to entire books of the Bible. She recites prayers. By the time she reaches her place of employment, she is ready for the day. "I turn my commute into my chapel."

Do something similar. Is there a block of time you can claim for God? Perhaps you could turn off the network news and open your Bible. Set the alarm fifteen minutes earlier. "If you abide in my word, you are truly my disciples, and you will know the truth, and the truth will set you free" (John 8:31–32 ESV). Free from fear. Free from dread. And, yes, free from anxiety.

GOD'S WORDS OF GOODNESS

"He is your praise, and He is your God, who has done for you these great and awesome things which your eyes have seen."

—*Deuteronomy 10:21*

Happy is the man who has the God of Jacob as his helper, whose hope is in the Lord his God—the God who made both earth and heaven, the seas and everything in them. He is the God who keeps every promise, who gives justice to the poor and oppressed and food to the hungry. He frees the prisoners and opens the eyes of the blind.

—*Psalm 146:5–8 TLB*

Come and see the works of God;
He is awesome in His doing toward the sons of men.

—*Psalm 66:5 NKJV*

As for God, His way is perfect;

The word of the LORD is proven;

He is a shield to all who trust in Him.

For who is God, except the LORD?

And who is a rock, except our God?

—*Psalm 18:30–31 NKJV*

JOURNALING GOD'S GOODNESS

1. What recent events have caused you to question God's timing— or doubt his goodness?

2. Write down a characteristic of God by each worry that can help you trust him in any circumstance.

3. How have you seen God's goodness in your life in the past few months?

4. What are some ways you can stand strong in the promises of God the next time doubt or anxiety hit?

Chapter 5

RECEIVE GOD'S MERCY

Remember the words of John's epistle: "If our heart condemns us, God is greater than our heart and knows all things" (1 John 3:20). When you feel unforgiven, evict the feelings. Emotions don't get a vote. Go back to Scripture. God's Word holds rank over self-criticism and self-doubt.

Fearless

THE VOICE YOU HEAR

Satan loves to dump buckets of diminishment and discouragement on us. He taunts us with the lie that we'll never overcome our bad habits and addictions. He specializes in telling us what we'll never do. But then God comes along, offering freedom with an even more powerful word: *nevertheless*.

Wouldn't you love God to write a *nevertheless* in your biography? Born to alcoholics, *nevertheless* she led a sober life. Never went to college, *nevertheless* he mastered a trade. Didn't read the Bible until retirement age, *nevertheless* he came to a deep and abiding faith.

We all need a *nevertheless*. And God has plenty to go around. Strongholds mean nothing to him. Remember Paul's words? "I use God's mighty weapons, not those made by men, to knock down the devil's strongholds" (2 Corinthians 10:4 TLB).

And it begins with us practicing the art of selective listening.

Two types of thoughts continuously vie for your attention. One says,

> WE ALL NEED A
> *NEVERTHELESS.* AND
> GOD HAS PLENTY
> TO GO AROUND.

"Yes, you can." The other says, "No, you can't." One says "God will help you." The other lies, "God has left you." One speaks the language of heaven; the other deceives in the vernacular of the enemy. One proclaims God's strengths; the other lists your failures. One longs to build you up; the other seeks to tear you down.

Here's the great news: you select the voice you hear. Why listen to the mockers? Why heed their voices? Why give ear to pea-brains and scoffers when you can, with the same ear, listen to the voice of God?

Turn a deaf ear to the old voices.

Open a wide eye to the new choices.

"God's power is very great for us who believe. That power is the same as the great strength God used to raise Christ from the dead and put him at his right side in the heavenly world" (Ephesians 1:19–20 NCV).

SURRENDER YOUR GUILT

*U*nresolved guilt will turn you into a miserable, weary, angry, stressed-out, fretful mess. In a psalm David probably wrote after his affair with Bathsheba, the king said:

> When I refused to confess my sin,
>> my body wasted away,
>> and I groaned all day long.
> Day and night your hand of discipline was heavy on me.
>> My strength evaporated like water in the summer heat.
>
> —Psalm 32:3–4 NLT

Guilt sucks the life out of our souls.
Grace restores it.

GUILT SUCKS THE LIFE OUT OF OUR SOULS. GRACE RESTORES IT.

The apostle Paul clung to this grace.

No one had more reason to feel the burden of guilt than Paul did. He was an ancient version of a terrorist, taking believers into custody and then spilling their blood. "Paul was like a wild man, going everywhere to devastate the believers, even entering private homes and dragging out men and women alike and jailing them" (Acts 8:3 TLB).

In addition, he was a legalist to the core. Before he knew Christ, Paul had spent a lifetime trying to save himself. His salvation depended on his perfection, on his performance.

> If anyone ever had reason to hope that he could save himself, it would be I. If others could be saved by what they are, certainly I could! For I went through the Jewish initiation ceremony when I was eight days old, having been born into a pure-blooded Jewish home that was a branch of the old original Benjamin family. So I was a real Jew if there ever was one! What's more, I was a member of the Pharisees who demand the strictest obedience to every Jewish law and custom. And sincere? Yes, so much so that I greatly persecuted the Church; and I tried to obey every Jewish rule and regulation right down to the very last point. (Philippians 3:4–6 TLB)

Paul had blood on his hands and religious diplomas on his wall.

But then came the Damascus road moment. Jesus appeared. Once Paul saw Jesus, he couldn't see anymore. He couldn't see value in his résumé anymore. He couldn't see merit in his merits or worth in his good works anymore. He couldn't see reasons to boast about anything he had done anymore. And he couldn't see any option except to spend the rest of his life talking less about himself and more about Jesus.

He became the great poet of grace. "But all these things that I once thought very worthwhile—now I've thrown them all away so that I can put my trust and hope in Christ alone" (Philippians 3:7 TLB).

In exchange for self-salvation, God gave Paul righteousness. "Now I am right with God, not because I followed the law, but because I believed in Christ" (Philippians 3:9 NCV).

Paul gave his guilt to Jesus. Period. He didn't numb it, hide it, deny it, offset it, or punish it. He simply surrendered it to Jesus.

As a result, Paul would later write, "I am still not all I should be, but I am bringing all my energies to bear on this one thing: Forgetting the past and looking forward to what lies ahead, I strain to reach the end of the race and receive the prize for which

God is calling us up to heaven because of what Christ Jesus did for us" (Philippians 3:13–14 TLB).

What would the apostle say to the guilt-laden? Simply this: "Rejoice in the Lord's mercy. Trust in his ability to forgive. Abandon any attempt at self-salvation or justification. No more hiding behind fig leaves. Cast yourself upon the grace of Christ and Christ alone."

> A HAPPY SAINT IS ONE WHO IS AT THE SAME TIME AWARE OF THE SEVERITY OF SIN AND THE IMMENSITY OF GRACE.

A happy saint is one who is at the same time aware of the severity of sin and the immensity of grace. Sin is not diminished, nor is God's ability to forgive it. The saint dwells in grace, not guilt. This is the tranquil soul.

As the heavens are

high above the earth,

so great is His *mercy*

toward those who fear Him;

as far as the east

is from the west,

so far has He *removed*

our transgressions from us.

PSALM 103:11–12

CLEAN YOUR LIFE LENS

*E*veryone has assumptions about life. Many are useful and constructive. We know that the sun will rise and set each day. We assume that storms will pass and that food is available in grocery stores. Some assumptions, however, are toxic. Even worse, they are contrary to the truth. A sampling of unhealthy assumptions would include:

I'm unworthy. I don't deserve to have good things happen to me.

People abandon me. When people come to know the real me, they leave.

It's all my fault. I'm to blame for every bad thing that happens to me.

No one has my back, which makes me vulnerable. Something bad is going to happen.

The world feels dangerous. I'm scared.

Many false beliefs were formed in the early years of our lives when we did not have the ability to challenge them. Their roots run deep. Yet such false assumptions create an anxiety-ridden life. God's solution? Truth. Face worries with truth. Bring "every thought into captivity to the obedience of Christ" (2 Corinthians 10:5 ASV). One way to do this is to correct faulty thinking with accurate thoughts.

I matter to God. He made me, knows me, and has a plan for my life.

I am worthy of love. I'm not perfect, but I have abilities and God-given gifts.

I'm not responsible for all the bad things. I've made mistakes, but I am learning and growing, and, most of all, I am forgiven by God.

I'm protected. It is a dangerous world, but I serve a mighty God who knows and loves me.

Listen to yourself. Monitor your beliefs about yourself, about God, and about the world. Don't allow false assumptions to take up any space in your mind. Immediately treat them with truth.

NAME THE PROBLEM

Hard as it may be, it's time to shine a light on that one weakness, bad habit, rotten attitude where Satan has a stronghold within you. Ah, there is the fitting word—*stronghold*: a fortress, citadel, thick walls, tall gates. It's as if the devil staked a claim on one weakness and constructed a rampart around it. "You ain't touching this flaw," he defies heaven, placing himself squarely between God's help and your

- explosive temper,
- fragile self-image,
- freezer-size appetite,
- distrust for authority.

Seasons come and go, and this Loch Ness monster still lurks in the water-bottom of your soul. He won't go away. He lives up to both sides of his name: strong enough to grip like a vise and stubborn enough to hold on.

It's time to defeat that monster. And it begins by naming it.

Think of the areas of your life in which you most need God's mercy.

Now try these steps:

Lay claim to the nearness of God.

> The LORD Almighty is with us;
>> The God of Jacob is our fortress.
>
> —*Psalm 46:7 NIV*

> "Never will I leave you;
>> never will I forsake you."
>
> —*Hebrews 13:5 NIV*

Cling to his character. The qualities of God—like his faithfulness, love, mercy, goodness—are the unchanging aspects of his character; they are also promises you can rely on in the midst of the change you desire in your life.

Confess your sins.

> If we confess our sins, he is faithful and just and will forgive us our sins and purify us from all unrighteousness.
>
> —*1 John 1:9 NIV*

Walk as a new creation.

> Therefore, if anyone is in Christ, the new creation has come: The old has gone, the new is here!
>
> —*2 Corinthians 5:17 NIV*

TAKEN AWAY

*D*enalyn and I enjoyed a nice dinner at a local restaurant the other night. About the same time we received our bill, we received a visit from a church member. He spotted us and came over to say hello. After we chatted for a moment, he reached down and took our bill and said, "I'll take this." (What a godly man.)

When he took it, guess what I did. I let him! I even ordered extra dessert. (Not really.) I just let him do what he wanted to do: I let him take it away.

Someday we will all stand before God. All of us will be present. All of us will have to give an account for our lives. Every thought, every deed, every action. Were it not for the grace of Christ, I would find this to be a terrifying thought.

Yet, according to Scripture, Jesus came to "take away the sins of the world" (John 1:29 Phillips). On the day when I appear before the judgment seat of God, I will point to Christ. When my list of sins is produced, I will gesture toward him and say, "He took it."

Let him take yours.

GOD'S WORDS OF MERCY

The LORD has heard my cry for mercy;
the LORD accepts my prayer.

—*Psalm 6:9 NIV*

"Go home to your own people and tell them how much
the Lord has done for you, and how he has had mercy
on you."

—*Mark 5:19 NIV*

"His mercy extends to those who fear him,
from generation to generation."

—*Luke 1:50 NIV*

[Christ] heals the brokenhearted
And binds up their wounds.

—*Psalm 147:3*

Despite all these things, overwhelming victory is ours
through Christ, who loved us.

—*Romans 8:37 NLT*

We have been sanctified through the offering of the
body of Jesus Christ once for all.

—*Hebrews 10:10*

JOURNALING ABOUT MERCY

1. God said he will remove our transgressions as far as the east is from the west (Psalm 103:11–12). What makes this promise seem either too good to be true . . . or not true for you?

2. What's holding you back from accepting God's mercy?

3. Imagine diving into an ocean that could wash away all your addictive and selfish behaviors. Describe how it would feel as those strongholds gave way and you rose up clean and forgiven.

Chapter 6

GET RID OF GUILT

*Don't fear God will discover your past. He already has.
Don't fear disappointing him in the future. He can show
you the chapter in which you will. With perfect knowledge
of the past and perfect vision of the future, he loves you
perfectly in spite of both.*

Come Thirsty

GUILTY CONSCIENCE

My hangover was terrible, but I could survive the headache.

The nausea was palpable, but I knew it would pass.

The discipline was severe, but I deserved it.

What I couldn't bear was the guilt.

I was taught from a young age that drunkenness is wrong. Our family tree is marked by a blight of alcoholism. My dad made it clear: alcohol abuse leads to trouble, and that trouble leads to misery. He regularly took me to rehab centers to visit his siblings for their benefit and mine. The battle of the bottle cost them their marriages, jobs, and health. More than once I promised that I would never get drunk.

Then why did I? Why did my friend and I, at the age of sixteen, get so ragingly inebriated that we could not drive? Why did we drive anyway? Why did I drink so much that I went to bed with head a-spinning and stomach a-turning? Why did I get so commode-hugging drunk that I could not stand?

Did I honestly think my dad wouldn't hear me throw up? (He did.) Did I think he would believe my excuse about Mexican food? (He didn't.) When I awoke the next morning, I had a pounding head, an angry father, and this: a guilty conscience.

There is a guilt that sits in the soul like a concrete block and causes a person to feel bad for being alive. There is a guilt that says, *I did bad*. And then there is a guilt that concludes: *I am bad*.

> THERE IS A GUILT THAT SAYS, *I DID BAD*. AND THEN THERE IS A GUILT THAT CONCLUDES: *I AM BAD*.

It was this deep, dark guilt that I felt. I found myself face-to-face with a version of me I had never known.

Maybe there is someone on the planet who has not known this quagmire of remorse, but I've never met that person.

Everyone stumbles.

The *difference* is in

the response. Some

stumble into the pit of

guilt. Others *tumble*

into the arms of God.

GLORY DAYS

ANTIDOTE TO GUILT

*O*ur guilt may be the result of a moment or a season in life. You failed as a parent. You blew it in your career. You squandered your youth or your money.

The result? Guilt.

A harsh consequence of the guilt? Anxiety.

Surprised? Lists of anxiety-triggers typically include busy schedules, unrealistic demands, or heavy traffic. But we must go deeper. Behind the frantic expressions on the faces of humanity is unresolved regret.

Indeed, humanity's first occasion of anxiety can be attributed to guilt.

"That evening [Adam and Eve] heard the sound of the Lord God walking in the garden; and they hid themselves among the trees" (Genesis 3:8 TLB).

What had happened to the first family? Until this point there was no indication they felt any fear or trepidation. They had never hidden from God. Indeed, they had nothing to hide. "The man and his wife were both naked, but they felt no shame" (Genesis 2:25 NLT).

But then came the serpent and the forbidden fruit. The first couple said yes to the serpent's temptation and no to God. And when they did, their world collapsed like an accordion. They scurried into the bushes and went into hiding, feeling a mélange of shame and dread. They did what anxious people do; they engaged in a flurry of cover-ups.

Can you relate? The only antidote to guilt is the power of God's grace. I could take you to the city, to the church within the city, to the section of seats within the church auditorium. I might be able to find the very seat in which I was sitting when this grace found me. I was a twenty-year-old college sophomore. For four years I had lived with the concrete block of guilt, not just from the first night of drunkenness but also a hundred more like it. The guilt had made a mess of my life, and I was headed toward a lifetime of misery. But then I heard a preacher

> I KNOW THE TRUTH FIRSTHAND: GUILT FRENZIES THE SOUL; GRACE CALMS IT.

do for me what I'm attempting to do for you: describe the divine grace that is greater than sin. When at the end of the message he asked if anyone would like to come forward and receive this grace, iron chains could not have held me back. Truth be told, chains had held me back. But mercy snapped the chains of guilt and set me free. I know this truth firsthand: guilt frenzies the soul; grace calms it.

UNHEALTHY WAYS WE

MANAGE GUILT

*H*ere's a Top-Ten List of how we try to deal with our guilt. See which sound a bit too familiar to you.

10. **Deny it.** Pretend we never stumbled. Concoct a plan to cover up the bad choice. One lie leads to another until we can no longer prolong the charade.

9. **Minimize it.** We didn't sin; we just lost our way, got caught up in the moment, or experienced a lapse in judgment.

8. **Bury it.** Suppress the guilt beneath a mound of work and a calendar of appointments. The busier we stay, the less time we spend with the people we have come to dislike most: ourselves.

7. **Punish it.** Beat ourselves up. Cut ourselves. Hurt ourselves. Priests used to flog themselves with whips. We've exchanged the whips for rules. More rules. Pray more! Study more! Give more! Show up earlier; stay up later.

6. **Numb it.** With a bottle of Grey Goose. With an hour

of Internet pornography. With a joint of marijuana, a rendezvous at the motel. Guilt disappears during happy hour, right? Funny how it reappears when we get home.

5. **Avoid the mention of it.** Just don't bring it up. Don't tell the family, the preacher, the buddies. Keep everything on the surface, and hope the Loch Ness monster of guilt lingers in the deep.

4. **Redirect it.** Lash out at the kids. Take it out on the spouse. Yell at the employees or the driver in the next lane.

3. **Offset it.** Never make another mistake. Seek perfection and expect it in others. Build the perfect family. The perfect career. Score perfect grades. Be the perfect Christian. And be absolutely intolerant of slipups or foul-ups by self or others.

2. **Normalize it.** Really, it's not that bad. Everyone else is doing the same . . . or worse. And after all, it helps us make it through the day.

1. **Embody it.** We didn't get drunk; we are drunks. We didn't screw up; we are screwups. We didn't just do bad; we are bad. Bad to the bone. We might even take pride in our badness. It's only a matter of time until we do something bad again.

REDEEMING THE STORY

When Joseph faced his brothers twenty years after they had betrayed him, he made an incredible proclamation. "As for you, you meant evil against me, but God meant it for good in order to bring about this present result, to preserve many people alive" (Genesis 50:20 NASB).

God is a Master Builder. This is the meaning behind Joseph's words "God meant it for good in order to *bring about . . .*" The Hebrew word translated here as *bring about* is a construction term.[7] It describes a task or building project akin to the one I drive through every morning. The state of Texas is rebuilding a highway overpass near my house. Three lanes have been reduced to one, transforming a morning commute into a daily stew. The interstate project, like human history, has been in development since before time began. Cranes hover overhead daily. Workers hold signs and shovels, and several thousand of us grumble. Well, at least I do. *How long is this going to last?*

My next-door neighbors have a different attitude toward the

project. The husband and wife are highway engineers, consultants to the department of transportation. They endure the same traffic jams and detours as the rest of us but do so with a better attitude. Why? They know how these projects develop. "It will take time," they respond to my grumbles, "but it will get finished. It's doable." They've seen the plans.

God is the Master Builder. He redeemed the story of Joseph. But we wonder if he will redeem our story as well?

Yes! Deliverance is to the Bible what jazz music is to Mardi Gras: bold, brassy, and

> IT WON'T BE PAINLESS. IT MAY NOT BE QUICK. BUT GOD WILL USE YOUR MESS FOR GOOD.

everywhere. It won't be painless. It may not be quick. But God will use your mess for good.

You are a version of Joseph in your generation. You carry something of God within you, something noble and holy, something the world needs—wisdom, kindness, mercy, skill. That is what God is building in you. But remember, "It will take time." Whether it's highways or hearts, that's just how these projects develop.

WAVE THE WHITE FLAG

*C*onfession is not complaining. If I merely recite my problems and tell you how tough my life is, I'm not confessing. Confession is not blaming. Pointing fingers at others without pointing any at myself may feel good for a while, but it does nothing to remove the conflict within me.

Confession is coming clean with God.

King David did. As if the affair with Bathsheba wasn't enough. As if the murder of her husband wasn't enough. Somehow David danced around the truth. He denied his wrong-doing for at least nine months until the child was born. It took a prophet to bring the truth to the surface, but when he did, David didn't like what he saw (2 Samuel 11:1–12:13).

He waved the white flag. No more combat with God. No more arguing with heaven. What was the result of such honesty?

> I confessed all my sins to you
> > and stopped trying to hide my guilt.
> I said to myself, "I will confess my rebellion to the LORD."
> > And you forgave me! All my guilt is gone. (Psalm 32:5 NLT)

GOD'S WORDS ON GUILT

But all these things that I [Paul] once thought very worthwhile—now I've thrown them all away so that I can put my trust and hope in Christ alone.

—*Philippians* 3:7 TLB

Now I am right with God, not because I followed the law, but because I believed in Christ.

—*Philippians* 3:9 NCV

I am still not all I should be, but I am bringing all my energies to bear on this one thing: Forgetting the past and looking forward to what lies ahead, I strain to reach the end of the race and receive the prize for which God is calling us up to heaven because of what Christ Jesus did for us.

—*Philippians* 3:13–14 TLB

The man and his wife were both naked, but they felt no shame.

—*Genesis* 2:25 NLT

Then I acknowledged my sin to you
    and did not cover up my iniquity.
I said, "I will confess
    my transgressions to the LORD."
And you forgave the
    guilt of my sin.

—*Psalm* 32:5 NIV

God's readiness to give and forgive is now public. Salvation's available for everyone!

—*Titus* 2:11 MSG

JOURNALING THROUGH GUILT

1. Think of some things from the past you still feel guilty about.

2. Release them, one by one, to the Father. What feeling is replacing the guilt?

3. Paul's statement challenges us to forget the past and look forward to what lies ahead. What are you looking forward to?

Chapter 7

SILENCE "IF ONLY"

Please underline this sentence: what you have in Christ is greater than anything you don't have in life. You have God, who is crazy about you, and the forces of heaven to monitor and protect you. You have the living presence of Jesus within you. In Christ you have everything.

Anxious for Nothing

THE GOOD LIFE

The widest river in the world is not the Mississippi, Amazon, or Nile. The widest river on earth is a body of water called If Only.

Throngs of people stand on its banks and cast longing eyes over the waters. They desire to cross but can't seem to find the ferry. They are convinced the If Only river separates them from the good life.

If only I were thinner, I'd have the good life.

If only I were richer, I'd have the good life.

If only the kids would come. If only the kids were gone. If only I could leave home, move home, get married, get divorced.

If only my skin were clear of pimples, my calendar free of people, my profession immune to layoffs, then I would have the good life.

The If Only river.

Are you standing on its shore? Does it seem the good life is always one *if only* away? One purchase away? One promotion away? One election, transition, or romance away?

If so, then we've traced your anxiety back to one of its

sources. You're in a hurry to cross the river and worried that you never will. Consequently, you work long hours, borrow more money, take on new projects, and pile on more responsibilities. Stress. Debt. Short nights. Long days. All part of the cost of the ticket to the land of the good life, right?

Not exactly, opined the apostle Paul. The good life begins, not when circumstances

> DOES IT SEEM THE GOOD LIFE IS ALWAYS ONE *IF ONLY* AWAY?

change, but when our attitude toward them does. Look again at his antidote for anxiety. "Be anxious for nothing, but in everything by prayer and supplication, with thanksgiving, let your requests be made known to God; and the peace of God, which surpasses all understanding, will guard your hearts and minds through Christ Jesus" (Philippians 4:6–7).

Paul embedded in the verses two essential words that deserve special attention: *with thanksgiving.* Sprinkled among your phrases "Help me . . . ," "Please give me . . . ," "If only . . ." should be two wonderful words: *Thank you.*

POLLYANNA OR CHICKEN LITTLE?

As we navigate life, it's easy to interpret problems and unmet desires through one of two extremes.

One extreme is the Chicken Little who runs around saying, "The sky is falling, the sky is falling." That's called panic.

The other extreme is Pollyanna, who says, "Oh, nothing bad is happening. It's all good." That's called ignorance.

The world stinks sometimes. There's cancer and there's death in this world. There's sadness in this world. There are orphans in this world. There's hunger in this world. And sometimes you're going to pray for things, and the prayer isn't going to be answered the way you want.

But somewhere between Chicken Little and Pollyanna are the sober, honest disciples of Christ who don't freak out at the presence of problems. Who don't lose faith when hard times come. Who don't make their contentment contingent on anything other than the presence of Christ.

When you stay on that path, you'll find the journey goes so much smoother.

WHAT'S NEXT

If only we could order life the way we order gourmet coffee. Wouldn't you love to mix and match the ingredients of your future?

"Give me a tall, extra-hot cup of adventure, cut the dangers, with two shots of good health."

"A decaf brew of longevity, please, with a sprinkle of fertility. Go heavy on the agility and cut the disability."

"I'll have the pleasure mocha with extra stirrings of indulgence. Make sure it's consequence free."

"I'll go with a grande happy-latte, with a dollop of love, sprinkled with Caribbean retirement."

Take me to that coffee shop. Too bad it doesn't exist. Truth is, life often hands us a concoction entirely different from the one we requested. Ever feel as though the barista-from-above called your name and handed you a cup of unwanted stress?

"Joe Jones, enjoy your early retirement. Looks as if it comes with marital problems and inflation."

"Mary Adams, you wanted four years of university education, then kids. You'll be having kids first. Congratulations on your pregnancy."

"A hot cup of job transfer six months before your daughter's graduation, Susie. Would you like some patience with that?"

Life comes caffeinated with surprises. Modifications. Transitions. Alterations. You move down the ladder, out of the house, over for the new guy, up through the system. All this moving. Some changes welcome, others not. We might request a decaffeinated life, but we don't get it. None of us pass through this life surprise free. If you don't want change, go to a soda machine; that's the only place you won't find any.

So make friends with whatever's next.

Embrace it. Accept it. Don't resist it. Change is not only a part of life; change is a *necessary* part of God's strategy. To use us to change the world, he alters our assignments. God transitioned Joseph from a baby brother to an Egyptian prince. He changed David from a shepherd to a king. Peter wanted to fish the Sea of Galilee. God called him to lead the first church.

> CHANGE IS NOT ONLY A PART OF LIFE; CHANGE IS A *NECESSARY* PART OF GOD'S STRATEGY.

God makes reassignments. Over time, we discover that the thing we thought we wanted is far less satisfying than what God has prepared for us.

What I have in

God is greater

than what I don't

have in this *life*.

TRAVELING LIGHT

GOD'S WORDS FOR IF ONLY

I have learned to be content whatever the circumstances. I know what it is to be in need, and I know what it is to have plenty. I have learned the secret of being content in any and every situation, whether well fed or hungry, whether living in plenty or in want. I can do all this through him who gives me strength.

—*Philippians 4:11–13* NIV

These little troubles are getting us ready for an eternal glory that will make all our troubles seem like nothing.

—*2 Corinthians 4:17* CEV

"Which of you by being anxious can add a cubit to his span of life? If then you are not able to do as small a thing as that, why are you anxious about the rest?"

—*Luke 12:25–26* RSV

Be strong and brave, and do the work. Don't be afraid or discouraged, because the LORD God, my God, is with you.

—1 Chronicles 28:20 NCV

Trust in the LORD with all your heart
    and lean not on your own understanding;
in all your ways submit to him,
    and he will make your paths straight.

—Proverbs 3:5–6 NIV

JOURNALING THROUGH IF ONLY

1. In what areas of your life does If Only tend to pop up? (Kids, finances, health, job, or some other area?)

2. Write five If Only statements you struggle with.

3. Now, one by one, give God each of those longings or fears.

4. What are some ways throughout your day you can turn from If Only to contentment in Christ?

Chapter 8

CATCH CALM

When the train goes through a tunnel and the world gets dark, do you jump out? Of course not. You sit still and trust the engineer to get you through.

—Corrie ten Boom
He Still Moves Stones

CALMING THE STORM

Nobody likes change . . . except babies. They cry for change.

The rest of us like small degrees of change but never dramatic, earth-rocking shifts of pattern and routines.

With change comes fear, insecurity, sorrow, and stress. What's the best solution? Hide and hope it all goes away? Never works. Change finds you.

It found the apostle Peter. He and his pals were sailing on calm waters when all of a sudden a storm hit. The winds changed. The waves rose. Not the kind of change a fisherman desires.

> During the fourth watch of the night Jesus went out to them, walking on the lake. When the disciples saw him walking on the lake, they were terrified. "It's a ghost," they said, and cried out in fear.
>
> But Jesus immediately said to them: "Take courage! It is I. Don't be afraid."
>
> "Lord, if it's you," Peter replied, "tell me to come to you on the water." (Matthew 14:25–28)

When he saw Jesus walking on the water, Peter decided to get a little change of scenery, to abandon the ship, and to step out in faith on the water.

The change worked.

"Come," he said.

Then Peter got down out of the boat, walked on the water and came toward Jesus. (v. 29)

It is possible to walk right over the storms of change. Peter proved it!

Unfortunately, one other thing changed Peter's mind.

But when he saw the wind, he was afraid and, beginning to sink, cried out, "Lord, save me!"

Immediately, Jesus reached out his hand and caught him. "You of little faith," he said, "why did you doubt?" (v. 30–31)

Peter's fear took over when his focus changed. When he saw Christ, he was strong. When he saw the storm, he wasn't.

If only Peter had focused on Christ . . . *Don't be afraid.*

If only Peter had trusted Jesus' command . . . *Come.*

If only Peter had stayed faithful . . . *Why doubt?*

Peter could have walked right over that sea of change.

One thing to remember: As Peter sank, he cried out, "Lord, save me!" (v. 30). He knew where to find help.

And Jesus reached out his hand to catch Peter.

That's another thing that never changes. Jesus is always there to pull us to safety.

> AS PETER SANK, HE CRIED OUT, "LORD, SAVE ME!" HE KNEW WHERE TO FIND HELP.

LOOK UP IN FAITH

We can calmly take our concerns to God because he is as near as our next breath!

This is the reassuring lesson from the miracle of the bread and fish. In an event crafted to speak to the anxious heart, Jesus told his disciples to do the impossible: feed five thousand people.

"Jesus lifted up His eyes, and seeing a great multitude coming toward Him, He said to Philip, 'Where shall we buy bread, that these may eat?' But this He said to test him, for He Himself knew what He would do" (John 6:5–6). When John described this gathering as a "great multitude," he was serious. There were five thousand men, plus women and children (Matthew 14:21). Imagine a capacity crowd at a sports arena, and you've got the picture. Jesus was willing to feed the entire crowd.

The disciples, on the other hand, wanted to get rid of everyone. "Send the multitudes away, that they may go into the villages and buy themselves food" (Matthew 14:15). Growling stomachs will soon become scowling faces, and the disciples might have a riot on their hands.

You aren't facing five thousand hungry bellies, but you are facing a deadline in two days . . . a loved one in need of a cure . . . a child who is being bullied at school . . . a spouse intertwined in temptation. On one hand you have a problem. On the other you have a limited quantity of wisdom, energy, patience, or time. What you have is nowhere near what you need. You have a thimbleful, and you need bucketloads. Typically you'd get anxious. You'd tell God to send the problem packing. "You've given me too much to handle, Jesus!"

This time, instead of starting with what you have, start with Jesus. Start with his wealth, his resources, and his strength. Before you open the ledger, open your heart. Before you count coins or count heads, count the number of times Jesus has helped you face the impossible. Before you lash out in fear, look up in faith. Take a moment. Turn to your Father for help.

> **BEFORE YOU LASH OUT IN FEAR, LOOK UP IN FAITH.**

CATCH YOUR BREATH

Time for rest must be taken on a daily and weekly basis. God told Moses, "Six days do your work, but on the seventh day do not work, so that your ox and your donkey may rest, and so that the slave born in your household and the foreigner living among you may be refreshed" (Exodus 23:12 NIV).

This was not a suggestion, recommendation, or piece of practical advice. This was a command. Rest! Once a week let the system reboot. Once a week let the entire household slow down. The Israelite who violated this law paid for the sin with his or her life. Today the death penalty is still in effect, but the death is a gradual one that comes from overwork, stress, and anxiety.

The Bible does not see rest as a sign of weakness or laziness but as a mark of reverence. To observe a Sabbath day of rest is to announce, "God knows what I need more than I do. If he says to rest, I will rest." And, as we do, our bodies and minds will be refreshed.

Never has rest been more important. We move at too fast a pace! Our adrenaline spigot is seldom shut off. As we race for late-night flights and add early-morning meetings, we are stretched beyond our limits. High adrenaline output depletes the brain's natural tranquilizers and sets the stage for high anxiety. Many of us have been trained to associate relaxation with irresponsibility, so some rewiring is needed.

Try this:

- Don't overdo it. Understand your limits. If you think you have no limits, then you have more than most people.
- Once you have reached your limits, stop. Don't work until you drop. Find a pace of life that works for you, and stick to it.
- Maintain regular breaks during the day. Naps are biblical.
- Give your mind a rest from technology. Turn off, unplug, detach from social media, news, and all the tech toys that deplete energy.
- Learn to relax. To relax is to disengage and let go. An hour or daylong Sabbath is not the time to catch up with your work. It is a time to entrust your work to God. After all, he worked for six days and then rested. The world didn't fall apart. It won't for you either.

PEACE DEPENDENT ON GOD

The disciples had every reason to feel unsettled. Then again, did they not have equal reason to feel at peace? By this point in their experience with Jesus, they had seen him

- heal leprosy (Matthew 8:3),
- heal the centurion's servant without going to the servant's bedside (Matthew 8:13),
- heal Peter's mother-in-law (Matthew 8:15),
- calm a violent sea (Matthew 8:26),
- heal a paralytic (Matthew 9:7),
- heal a woman who had been sick for twelve years (Matthew 9:22),
- raise a girl from the dead (Matthew 9:25),
- drive out an evil spirit (Mark 1:25),
- heal a demon-possessed man in a cemetery (Mark 5:15),
- change water into wine (John 2:9), and
- heal a man who had been an invalid for thirty-eight years (John 5:9).

If your peace is contingent upon circumstances, you open the door to anxiety and fear. Peace 101 says that God is greater than your challenges. When the world throws challenges your way, you can choose to catch calm rather than worry.

Your peace does not depend upon people, which is good because they are fickle. Your peace does not depend upon the government, which is good because rulers come and go. Your peace does not even depend upon a peaceful home, which is good because kids tend to misbehave. Peace—long-lasting peace—depends only upon God.

The boss put me in a bad mood. No he didn't. You put yourself in a bad mood.

This situation has me frazzled and out-of-sorts. No it hasn't. You've let the situation pull you down.

The kids are making me irritable. They may be misbehaving, but no one can make you irritable without your permission.

With Jesus Christ living within you by the power of his Holy Spirit, you can take control of your thoughts before they take control of you. Remember, "the Spirit who lives in you is greater than the spirit who lives in the world" (1 John 4:4 NLT).

Take a deep breath and relax. Anxiety is needless when God is near.

CARRY ON

In the days leading up to the war with Germany, the British government commissioned a series of posters. The idea was to capture encouraging slogans on paper and distribute them about the country. Capital letters in a distinct typeface were used, and a simple two-color format was selected. The only graphic was the crown of King George VI.

The first poster was distributed in September of 1939:

YOUR COURAGE
YOUR CHEERFULNESS
YOUR RESOLUTION
WILL BRING
US VICTORY

Soon thereafter a second poster was produced:

FREEDOM IS
IN PERIL
DEFEND IT
WITH ALL
YOUR MIGHT

These two posters appeared up and down the British countryside. On railroad platforms and in pubs, stores, and restaurants. They were everywhere. A third poster was created yet never distributed. More than 2.5 million copies were printed yet never seen until nearly sixty years later when a bookstore owner in northeast England discovered one in a box of old books he had purchased at an auction. It read:

KEEP
CALM
AND
CARRY
ON

The poster bore the same crown and style of the first two posters. It was never released to the public, however, but was held in reserve for an extreme crisis, such as an invasion by Germany. The bookstore owner framed it and hung it on the wall. It became so popular that the bookstore began producing identical images of the original design on coffee mugs, postcards, and posters. Everyone, it seems, appreciated the reminder from another generation to keep calm and carry on.[9]

God's sovereignty doesn't negate our responsibility. Just the opposite. It empowers it. When we trust God, we think more clearly and react more decisively. Like Nehemiah, who said, "We prayed to our God and posted a guard day and night to meet this threat" (Nehemiah 4:9 NIV).

We prayed . . . and posted. We trusted and acted. Trust God to do what you can't. Obey God, and do what you can.

Don't let the crisis paralyze you. Don't let the sadness overwhelm you. Don't let the fear intimidate you. To do nothing is the wrong thing. To do something is the right thing. And to believe is the highest thing. Just . . .

KEEP

CALM

AND

CARRY

ON

OPEN DOORS

Jesus is a doorman. He opens and shuts doors all the time, and no one can close what he has opened, and no one can open what he has closed. He stands at the doors and knocks (Revelation 3:20). If they are locked, he has a key (Revelation 3:7–8). If he doesn't want to use the key, he walks through the walls (John 20:19). But better than being just a doorman, Jesus is the door! (John 10:9 NCV).

So what is Jesus trying to say with all this talk about doors? He controls all gateways and passages from one place to another. Nothing gets past him without his knowing it.

Jesus doesn't leave us standing in the hallway or outside in the cold. He has something for us—new opportunities, new destinations, new chances to show our faith in him.

What do we do as we wait for other doors to open? In the book of Revelation (3:7–8), Jesus makes it clear to the church of Philadelphia—keep God's Word and commands, stay faithful, and don't curse or deny him.

Right now Jesus is sorting through that vast key ring, looking for the right door for you. He may have to lock and unlock a few other doors first, but one is sure to open soon. Trust him.

GOD'S WORDS OF CALM

"Do not be afraid . . . I am your shield, your exceedingly great reward."

—*Genesis 15:1*

"Do not be afraid, for I am with you."

—*Genesis 26:24* NLT

"Do not be afraid; do not be discouraged, for the LORD your God will be with you wherever you go."

—*Joshua 1:9* NIV

"Do not be afraid; God has heard."

—*Genesis 21:17* NIV

The LORD is with me; I will not be afraid.
What can mere mortals do to me?

—*Psalm 118:6* NIV

The disciples heard it . . . and were greatly afraid. But Jesus came and touched them and said, "Arise, and do not be afraid."

—*Matthew 17:6–7*

JOURNALING CALM

1. What situations cause you to lose your calm most often?

2. In those moments, think about the source of your anxiety. Why do you feel it is all up to you . . . or that God won't come through?

3. Write the following Scripture and place it on your bathroom mirror or desk: "Do not be afraid; do not be discouraged, for the LORD your God will be with you wherever you go" (Joshua 1:9 NIV). The next time you sense calm is giving way to anxiety, speak this promise out loud as you personalize it to your situation: "I will not be afraid or discouraged when I face _____ , Father, because you will be with me."

Chapter 9

PRACTICE GRATITUDE

It's essential for us to celebrate God's blessings. Declare with David: "[I will] daily add praise to praise. I'll write the book on your righteousness, talk up your salvation the livelong day, never run out of good things to write or say" (Psalm 71:14–15 MSG).

Fearless

COUNT YOUR BLESSINGS

*G*ratitude is a mindful awareness of the benefits of life. It is the greatest of virtues. Studies have linked the emotion with a variety of positive effects. Grateful people tend to be more empathetic and forgiving of others. People who keep a gratitude journal are more likely to have a positive outlook on life. Grateful individuals demonstrate less envy, materialism, and self-centeredness. Gratitude improves self-esteem and enhances relationships, quality of sleep, and longevity.[10] If it came in pill form, gratitude would be deemed the miracle cure. It's no wonder, then, that God's anxiety therapy includes a large, delightful dollop of gratitude.

My friend Jerry has taught me the value of gratitude. He is seventy-eight years old and regularly shoots his age on the golf course. (If I ever do the same, I'll need to live to be a hundred.) His dear wife, Ginger, battles Parkinson's disease. What should have been a wonderful season of retirement has been

> GOD'S ANXIETY THERAPY INCLUDES A LARGE, DELIGHTFUL DOLLOP OF GRATITUDE.

marred by multiple hospital stays, medication, and struggles. Many days she cannot keep her balance. Jerry has to be at her side. Yet he never complains. He always has a smile and a joke. And he relentlessly beats me in golf. I asked Jerry his secret. He said, "Every morning Ginger and I sit together and sing a hymn. I ask her what she wants to sing. She always says, 'Count Your Blessings.' So we sing it. And we count our blessings."

> WORRY REFUSES TO SHARE THE HEART WITH GRATITUDE.

Take a moment and follow Jerry's example. Look at your blessings.

Do you see any friends? Family? Do you see any grace from God? The love of God? Do you see any gifts? Abilities or talents? Skills?

As you look at your blessings, take note of what happens. Anxiety grabs his bags and slips out the back door. Worry refuses to share the heart with gratitude. One heartfelt thank-you will suck the oxygen out of worry's world. So say it often. Focus more on what you do have and less on what you don't. It's true. Gratitude is the secret to a life of contentment.

POSTURE OF GRATITUDE

God provides so many ways for us to grow in gratitude. Unfortunately, our attempts often tend to follow this pattern:

- Take a few moments to sit and look around you.
- Find something negative in everything you see.
- Make a list of all the critical and unhappy thoughts that come into your mind.
- Notice how you feel when you are finished, and write those feelings down.

Not much fun. A steady diet of critical, negative, and ungrateful thoughts leaves us critical, negative, and ungrateful. Now try the opposite approach.

- Take a few moments and look around you.
- Find something positive in everything you see.
- Make a list of all the kind, generous, and grateful thoughts that come into your mind.
- Notice the difference.

What if this exercise became a way of life? It can. Nobody other than you has the power to make you miserable and unhappy. As you pass through your day, look for opportunities to see the good in the world, in nature, and in life. This simple exercise will place your mind in a healthy posture of gratitude.

Gratitude always

leaves us *looking*

to God and away from dread.

It does to anxiety what

the *morning* sun does to

valley mist. It burns it up.

YOU'LL GET THROUGH THIS

FOCUS ON THE PRESENT

Have you ever left an appliance at the repair shop? Perhaps your toaster broke or your microwave oven stopped working. You tried to fix it but had no success. So you took it to the specialist. You explained the problem and then . . .

- offered to stay and help him fix it,
- hovered next to his workbench asking questions about the progress,
- threw a sleeping bag on the floor of the workshop so you could watch the repairman at work.

If you did any of these things, you don't understand the relationship between client and repairman. The arrangement is uncomplicated. Leave it with him to fix it. Our protocol with God is equally simple. Leave your problem with him. "I know whom I have believed and am persuaded that He is able to keep what I have committed to Him until that Day" (2 Timothy 1:12).

God does not need our help, counsel, or assistance. (Please repeat this phrase: I hereby resign as ruler of the universe.) When he is ready for us to reengage, he will let us know.

Until then, replace anxious thoughts with grateful ones. God takes thanksgiving seriously.

Here's why: gratitude keeps us focused on the present.

The Bible's most common word for *worry* is the Greek term *merimnate*. The origin is *merimna* . This is a compound of a verb and a noun. The verb is *divide*. The noun is *mind*. To be anxious, then, is to divide the mind.[11] Worry takes a meat cleaver to our thoughts, energy, and focus. Anxiety chops up our attention. It sends our awareness in a dozen directions.

> WORRY TAKES A MEAT CLEAVER TO OUR THOUGHTS, ENERGY, AND FOCUS. ANXIETY CHOPS UP OUR ATTENTION.

We worry about the past—what we said or did. We worry about the future—tomorrow's assignments or the next decade's developments. Anxiety takes our attention from the right now and directs it "back then" or "out there."

But when you aren't focused on your problem, you have a sudden availability of brain space. Use it for good.

EACH DAY IS A GIFT

I was flying home from the Midwest when a snowstorm delayed my arrival in Dallas. I raced to the gate in hopes of catching the final flight of the night for San Antonio. The airport was in a state of contained turmoil, everyone dashing to a gate. The airline had already loaded extra passengers on my plane. With all the charm I could muster, I asked the attendant, "Are any seats left?"

She looked at her computer screen. "No," she replied, "I'm afraid . . ."

I just knew how she was going to finish the sentence: "I'm afraid you'll have to spend the night here." "I'm afraid you'll need to find a hotel." "I'm afraid you'll have to catch the 6:00 a.m. flight to San Antonio."

But she said none of these. Instead, she looked up and smiled. "I'm afraid there are no more seats in coach. We are going to have to bump you up to first class. Do you mind if we do that?"

"Do you mind if I kiss you?" So I boarded the plane and nestled down in the wide seat with the extra legroom.

Color me thankful.

Not every passenger was as appreciative as I was. A fellow across the aisle from me was angry because he had only one pillow. With the attendants scrambling to lock doors and prepare for the delayed departure, he was complaining about the insufficient service. "I paid extra to fly first class. I am accustomed to better attention. I want another pillow!"

On the other side of the aisle, yours truly smiled like a guy who had won the lottery without buying a ticket. One passenger grumbled; the other was grateful. The difference? The crank paid his way into first class. My seat was a gift.

If you feel the world owes you something, brace yourself for a life of sour hours. The grateful heart, on the other hand, sees each day as a gift.

THANKFUL PEOPLE FOCUS LESS ON THE PILLOWS THEY LACK AND MORE ON THE PRIVILEGES THEY HAVE.

Thankful people focus less on the pillows they lack and more on the privileges they have.

On which side of the aisle do you find yourself?

THANK YOU, GOD

The grateful heart is like a magnet sweeping over the day, collecting reasons for gratitude. A zillion diamonds sparkle against the velvet of your sky each night. *Thank you, God.* A miracle of muscles enables your eyes to read these words and your brain to process them. *Thank you, God.* Your heart will beat about three billion times in your lifetime. *Thank you, God.*

For the jam on our toast and the milk on our cereal. For the blanket that calms us and the joke that delights us and the warm sun that reminds us of God's love. For the men who didn't cheat on their wives, and the wives who didn't turn from their men, and the kids who, in spite of unspeakable pressure to dishonor their parents decided not to do so. *Thank you, Lord.*

GRATITUDE GETS US THROUGH THE HARD STUFF.

Gratitude gets us through the hard stuff. To reflect on your blessings is to rehearse God's accomplishments. To rehearse God's accomplishments is to discover his heart. To discover his heart is to discover not just good gifts but the good Giver.

GOD'S WORDS ABOUT GRATITUDE

God is able to make all grace abound toward you, that
you, always having all sufficiency in all things, may have
an abundance for every good work.

—2 Corinthians 9:8

God is sheer mercy and grace;
    not easily angered, he's rich in love.

—Psalm 103:8 MSG

By grace you have been saved through faith . . . it is the
gift of God.

—Ephesians 2:8

We are God's masterpiece. He has created us anew in Christ Jesus, so we can do the good things he planned for us long ago.

—*Ephesians 2:10* NLT

Hope in the LORD;
For with the LORD there is mercy,
And with Him is abundant redemption.

—*Psalm 130:7*

Let all those who seek You rejoice and be glad in You;
Let such as love Your salvation say continually,
"The LORD be magnified!"

—*Psalm 40:16*

JOURNALING GRATITUDE

1. Do you recall a time when you were overwhelmed with gratitude to God? How did you give concrete form to your gratitude through your words and actions?

2. Why was it important that you expressed your gratitude in those ways? What might you and others have missed if you hadn't shown thankfulness as you did?

3. We can't *name*—express gratitude—until we *notice*. How would you categorize your posture of gratitude in your current season of life?

Chapter 10

PRAY HIS PEACE

The path to peace is paved with prayer. As you pray, the peace of God will guard your heart and mind. You may be facing the perfect storm, but Jesus offers the perfect peace.

Anxious for Nothing

173

HOLD ON

*P*aradise is not promised until Jesus returns. Peace, joy, and the absence of pain are promises of the future, not the present. Sin is still epidemic. But the cure is coming.

Remember that *Christ predicted the bad news*. Christ forewarned us about spiritual bailouts, ecological turmoil, and worldwide persecution. He told us things are going to get bad, really bad, before they get better. And when conditions worsen, "See to it that you are not alarmed" (Matthew 24:6 NIV). Jesus chose a stout term for *alarmed* that he used on no other occasion. It means "to wail, to cry aloud," as if Jesus counseled the disciples, "Don't freak out when bad stuff happens."

The only time we should get scared is when something surprises God. If something takes God by surprise, we are doomed. Since God knows all things, we are comforted.

If Christ can predict the problem, he can solve it. The same God who has the power of omniscience (knowing everything at every time) also has the power of omnipresence (being multipresent) and omnipotence (having all power). That trinitarian trifecta is unstoppable. All problems are too small in the shadow of God.

Take comfort; it's the beginning of the end and the beginning of the new beginning. In Matthew 24:8, Jesus called these challenges birth pangs. Birth pangs must occur before a new birth. During this time the mother keeps focused on the end result, the moment she gets to hold that beautiful baby in her arms. She knows birth pangs don't last forever and they signal a new beginning in her life. Calamities and catastrophes are the earthly pains that must occur before the birth of the new world. Hold on.

> CALAMITIES AND CATASTROPHES ARE THE EARTHLY PAINS THAT MUST OCCUR BEFORE THE BIRTH OF THE NEW WORLD.

HEAVENLY HELPERS

The prophet Daniel discovered how seriously God takes our prayers—even when it may not at first seem that way. He was troubled. He resolved to pray. After three weeks (so much for one-shot attempts at prayer), Daniel saw a man dressed in linen with a belt of gold around his waist. His body was like topaz, his face like lightning, his eyes on fire. His arms and legs resembled burnished bronze. His voice was like the roar of a multitude (Daniel 10:5–6 NIV).

Daniel was so stunned he fell to the ground. The angel said:

Don't be afraid, Daniel. Since the first day you began to pray for understanding and to humble yourself before your God, your request has been heard in heaven. I have come in answer to your prayer. But for twenty-one days the spirit prince of the kingdom of Persia blocked my way. Then Michael, one of the archangels, came to help me, and I left him there with the spirit prince of the kingdom of Persia. Now I am here to explain what will happen to your people in the future." (Daniel 10:12–14 NLT)

The moment Daniel began praying, the answer was issued. Demonic forces blocked the pathway of the angel. The impasse lasted a full three weeks until the archangel Michael arrived on the scene with his superior authority. The standoff was ended, and the prayer was answered.

Have your prayers been met with a silent sky? Have you prayed and heard nothing? Are you floundering in the land between an offered and an answered prayer?

If so, I beg you, don't give up. What the angel said to Daniel, God says to you: "Since the first day that you set your mind to gain understanding and to humble yourself before your God, your words were heard" (Daniel 10:12 NIV). You have been heard in heaven. Angelic armies have been dispatched. Reinforcements have been rallied. God promises, "I will contend with him who contends with you" (Isaiah 49:25).

Keep praying. Heaven has helpers for you.

> ARE YOU FLOUNDERING IN THE LAND BETWEEN AN OFFERED AND AN ANSWERED PRAYER?

Pray! Since God works, prayer works. Since God is good, *prayer* is good. Since you matter to God, your prayers matter in *heaven*. You're never without hope because you're never without prayer.

BEFORE AMEN

PRAYERS FOR PEACE

Worry happens when we keep our problems to ourselves or present our problems to the puny deities of money, muscle, or humankind. The act of prayer moves us from a spirit of concern to a spirit of gratitude. Even before our prayers are answered, our hearts begin to change. So take these steps:

Take your worries to God. Set aside some time each day to pour out your concerns, complaints, fears, and woes to him. Tell him what is keeping you awake. Don't suppress; express! If you find yourself worrying about something during the day, write it down so you can bring it up in your next prayer session. Take everything to God and then . . . leave it with him. When the intrusive thought reenters your mind, just tell yourself, *I left that one with God.*

Find a promise to match your problem. Populate your prayers with "You said . . . ." "You said you would walk me through the waters" (see Isaiah 43:2). "You said you would lead me through the valley" (see Psalm 23:4). "You said you would never leave or forsake me" (see Hebrews 13:5). Spend time in the promises and stories of Scripture. Find a promise that fits your problem, and build your prayer around it. These prayers of faith touch the heart of God and activate the angels of heaven. Miracles are set into motion. Your answer may not come overnight, but it will come. And you will overcome.

Pray specifically. Many of our anxieties are threatening because they are ill-defined and vague. Tell God exactly what troubles you, so that when he answers the prayer, you will know. Generic prayers aren't nearly as effective as heartfelt prayers that target particular needs.

Peace happens when we pray. Try it now with whatever is weighing your heart down. You'll be glad you did.

PEACE IN GOD'S PRESENCE

All people can enjoy God's presence. But many don't. They plod through life as if there were no God to love them. As if their only strength was their own. As if the only solution comes from within, not above. They live God-less lives.

But there are those among us who sense, see, and hear the presence of God. People who pursue God as Moses did. When suddenly tasked with the care of two million ex-slaves, the liberator began to wonder, *How am I going to provide for these people? How will we defend ourselves against enemies? How can we survive?* Moses needed supplies, managers, equipment, and experience. But when Moses prayed for help, he declared, "If Your Presence does not go with us, do not bring us up from here" (Exodus 33:15).

Moses preferred to go nowhere with God than anywhere without him.

Do likewise. Make God's presence your passion. How?

MOSES PREFERRED TO GO NOWHERE WITH GOD THAN ANYWHERE WITHOUT HIM.

Be more sponge and less rock. Place a rock in the ocean, and what happens? Its surface gets wet. The exterior may change color, but the interior remains untouched. Yet place a sponge in the ocean, and notice the change. It absorbs the water. The ocean permeates every pore and alters the essence of the sponge.

God surrounds us the same way the Pacific surrounds an ocean floor pebble. He is everywhere—above, below, on all sides. We choose our response—rock or sponge? Resist or receive. Everything within you says harden the heart. Run from God; resist God; blame God. But be careful. Hard hearts never heal. Spongy ones do. Open every pore of your soul to God's presence.

Pray to God. Lean into his promises. Pursue his peace. Know that he not only hears, but is actively and intimately involved in your specific situation. Your family may be gone. Your supporters may have left. Your counselor may be silent. But God has not budged. His promise still stands: "I am with you and will watch over you wherever you go" (Genesis 28:15 NIV).

UNCEASING PRAYER

Unceasing prayer may sound complicated, but it needn't be that way.

Do this. Change your definition of prayer. Think of prayer less as an activity for God and more as an awareness of God. Seek to live in uninterrupted awareness. Acknowledge his presence everywhere you go.

As you stand in line to register your car, think, *Thank you, Lord, for being here*. In the grocery store as you shop, think, *Your presence, my King, I welcome*. As you wash the dishes, worship your Maker. Brother Lawrence did. This well-known saint called himself the "lord of all pots and pans." In his book *The Practice of the Presence of God*, he wrote:

> The time of business does not with me differ from the time of prayer; and in the noise and clatter of my kitchen, while several persons are at the same time calling for different things, I possess God in as great tranquility as if I were upon my knees at the blessed sacrament.[12]

Besides, it makes more sense to talk to God than mumble to yourself.

People struggle with life when they don't have answers. The darkest valleys are blackened by the shadow of question marks. So what do you do? Think harder? Try harder? Hold longer conversations with yourself? Why not pray to the One with all the answers and let him take over?

> UNCEASING PRAYER MAY SOUND COMPLICATED, BUT IT NEEDN'T BE THAT WAY.

GOD'S WORDS OF PEACE

Prayer is essential in this ongoing warfare. Pray hard and long. Pray for your brothers and sisters.

—*Ephesians 6:18* MSG

The peace of God, which surpasses all understanding, will guard your hearts and minds through Christ Jesus.

—*Philippians 4:7*

"Peace I leave with you; my peace I give you. I do not give to you as the world gives. Do not let your hearts be troubled and do not be afraid."

—*John 14:27* NIV

God is not the author of confusion but of peace, as in all
the churches of the saints.

—*1 Corinthians 14:33*

I sought the LORD, and He answered me,
And delivered me from all my fears.

—*Psalm 34:4* NASB

"Whatever you ask in My name, that will I do, so that
the Father may be glorified in the Son."

—*John 14:13* NASB

JOURNALING PEACE

1. When do you most feel God's peace?

2. How could you arrange your day to spend even more time pursuing God and his peace?

3. Ponder this passage: Jesus said, "Peace I leave with you; my peace I give you. I do not give to you as the world gives. Do not let your hearts be troubled and do not be afraid" (John 14:27 NIV). Which words in this verse have special meaning for you? Why?

CONCLUSION

God meets needs daily. Not weekly or annually. He will give us what we need when it is needed.

But how fast we forget that in the middle of life's storms. Perhaps that's why I wrote this resolve:

Today, I will live today.
Yesterday has passed.
Tomorrow is not yet.
I'm left with today.
So, today, I will live today.
Relive yesterday? No.
I will learn from it.
I will seek mercy for it.
I will take joy in it.
But I won't live in it.
The sun has set on yesterday.
The sun has yet to rise on tomorrow.
Worry about the future? To what gain?

It deserves a glance, nothing more.
I can't change tomorrow until tomorrow.
Today, I will live today.
I will face today's challenges with today's strength.
I will dance today's waltz with today's music.
I will celebrate today's opportunities with today's hope.
Today.

A new day awaits you, my friend. A new season in which you will worry less and trust more. A season with reduced fear and enhanced faith. Can you imagine a life in which you are anxious for nothing? In which you can trade your cares for calm? God can. And with his help, you will experience it.

SOURCES

Adapted from previously published material in *Anxious for Nothing* (Thomas Nelson, 2017): ix–xi, 2–3, 4–5, 6–7, 14, 28-29, 30, 46–47, 54, 60–61, 72, 82–85, 92, 100–101, 108–109, 138–140, 156–157, 162–163, 176–177, 180–181, 191–192

Adapted from previously published material in *Facing Your Giants* (Thomas Nelson, 2006): 80–81, 90–91

Adapted from previously published material in *Fearless* (Thomas Nelson, 2009): 20–21, 32–33, 34, 124–125

Adapted from previously published material in *Max on Life* (Thomas Nelson, 2011): 40–41, 46–47, 112, 122, 134–136, 148, 174–175, 184–185

Adapted from previously published material in *3:16: The Numbers of Hope* (Thomas Nelson, 2006): 64

Adapted from previously published material in *Traveling Light* (Thomas Nelson, 2006): 191–192

Adapted from previously published material in *You'll Get Through This* (Thomas Nelson, 2015: 10–11, 52–53, 66–67, 70–71, 104–106, 110–111, 144–146, 164–165, 166, 182–183

NOTES

1. Henri J. M. Nouwen, *The Essential Henri Nouwen*, ed. Robert A. Jonas (Boston: Shambhala, 2009),131–32.
2. Miller, Joel, "The Secret behind the Bible's most highlighted verse." *Theology That Sticks*, August 4, 2015.
3. Taylor Clark, "It's Not the Job Market: The Three Real Reasons Why Americans Are More Anxious Than Ever Before," *Slate*, January 31, 2011, http://www.slate.com/articles/arts/culturebox/2011/01 /its_not_the_job_market.html.
4. C. S. Lewis, *Prince Caspian: The Return to Narnia* (New York: Macmillan Publishing, 1951), 136. Copyright © C. S. Lewis Pte. Ltd. 1942, 1943, 1944, 1952. Extract reprinted by permission.
5. "Texas investors build $300 Million Luxury Bunker Community for Doomsday Scenario," *Associated Press*, November 11, 2016.
6. Christyn Taylor, CaringBridge.org, August 22, 2010, created at http:// www.caringbridge.org/visit/rebeccataylor1. Used by permission.
7. Kent and Amber Brantly with David Thomas, *Called for Life: How Loving Our Neighbor Led Us into the Heart of the Ebola Epidemic* (Colorado Springs, CO: WaterBrook, 2015), 115.

8. The same term is used in Genesis 13:4 ("he had . . . *built* an alter" [NIV]), Job 9:9 ("He *made* the Bear"), and Proverbs 8:26 ("he *made* the earth" [NIV]).

9. "The Story of Keep Calm and Carry On," YouTube video, 3:01, posted by Temujin Doran, www.youtube.com/watch/v=FrHkKXFRb CI&sns=fb. See also *Keep Calm and Carry On: Good Advice for Hard Times* (Kansas City, MO: Andrew McMeel, 2009), introduction.

10. Kennon M. Sheldon, Todd B. Kashdan, and Michael F. Steger, eds., *Designing Positive Psychology: Taking Stock and Moving Forward* (New York: Oxford University Press, 2011), 249–54. See also Amit Amin, "The 31 Benefits of Gratitude You Didn't Know About: How Gratitude Can Change Your Life," Happier Human, http://happierhuman.com/benefits-of-gratitude/.

11. Spiros Zodhiates, ed., *Hebrew-Greek Key Word Study Bible: Key Insights into God's Word, New International Version* (Chattanooga, TN: AMG Publishers, 1996), #3534, p. 2093.

12. Brother Lawrence, *The Practice of the Presence of God* (Old Tappan, NJ: Revell, 1958), 9.

If you enjoyed this book
or it has touched your life in some way,
we'd love to hear from you.

Please write a review at Hallmark.com,
e-mail us at booknotes@hallmark.com,
or send your comments to:

Hallmark Book Feedback
P.O. Box 419034
Mail Drop 100
Kansas City, MO 64141